GROUNDBREAKERS

Hernán Cortés

Brendan January

Heinemann Library
Chicago, Illinois

© 2003 Reed Educational & Professional Publishing
Published by Heinemann Library,
an imprint of Reed Educational & Professional Publishing,
Chicago, Illinois

Customer Service 888-454-2279

Visit our website at www.heinemannlibrary.com

Page layout and maps by 3 Loop 9, Los Angeles, CA
Photo research by Bill Broyles
Printed in the United States by Lake Book Manufacturing, Inc.

07 06 05 04 03
10 9 8 7 6 5 4 3 2 1

Library of Congress Cataloging-in-Publication Data
January, Brendan, 1972-
   Hernán Cortés / Brendan January.
      p. cm. -- (Groundbreakers)
Includes bibliographical references and index.
   ISBN 1-4034-0243-4 (lib. bdg.) -- ISBN 1-4034-0479-8 (pbk.)
   1. Cortés, Hernán, 1485-1547--Juvenile literature. 2.
Mexico--History--Conquest, 1519-1540--Juvenile literature. 3.
Conquerors--Mexico--Biography--Juvenile literature. I. Title. II.
Series.
   F1230.C835 J36 2002
   972'.02'092--dc21

2002008342

Acknowledgments
The author and publishers are grateful to the following for permission to reproduce copyright material:
p. 4 Academia BB AA S Fernando Madrid/Dagli Orti/Art Archive; p. 5 Museo degli Argenti, Florence/Bridgeman Art Library; p. 6 Vanni/Art Resource; p. 7 Dagli Orti/Art Archive; pp. 8, 11, 19, 21, 23, 24, 25, 28, 30, 32, 35, 38, 39 North Wind Picture Archives; p. 9 Musée de la Marine, Paris/Dagli Orti/Art Archive; p. 10 Doug Scott/Age Fotostock; p. 12 National Palace, Mexico City/Dagli Orti/Art Archive; pp. 13, 37 The Granger Collection, New York; p. 14 Biblioteca Nacional Madrid/Dagli Orti/Art Archive; p. 15 Biblioteca Nazionale Centrale, Florence, Italy/Bridgeman Art Library; p. 16 Antochiw Collection, Mexico/Mireille Vautier/Art Archive; pp. 17, 36 Charles & Josette Lenars/Corbis; p. 18 Museum für Völkerkunde, Vienna/Dagli Orti/Art Archive; p. 20 Army Museum, Madrid/Dagli Orti/Art Archive; p. 22 Look GMBH/eStock Photos; p. 27 Werner Forman/Art Resource; p. 31 Joseph Martin/Art Archive; p. 34 British Embassy, Mexico City, Mexico/Bridgeman Art Library; p. 33 Museo Nazionale Preistorico Etnografico Luigu Pigoroni, Rome/Werner Forman/Art Resource; p. 40 Archivo Iconografico, S.A./Corbis; p. 41 Scala/Art Resource

Cover photograph: Giraudon/Art Resource

Some words are shown in bold, **like this.** You can find out what they mean by looking in the glossary.

Contents

Who Was Hernán Cortés?

On November 8, 1519, Hernán Cortés experienced his greatest moment. Over the past year, he had sailed from Cuba to Mexico and had led his army more than 200 miles (322 kilometers) into the Mexican countryside. During the journey, he had fought battles, made friends, and bullied and flattered local chiefs. He also heard stories of the powerful Aztec **empire,** its heaps of gold, and its glorious capital city beyond the mountains, Tenochtitlán. Now, he stood at the gates of Tenochtitlán and addressed the city's ruler, Montezuma.

"Is it really you?" asked Cortés. "Are you truly Montezuma?"

Filled with emotion, Cortés went to embrace the **emperor,** but he was stopped by Montezuma's servants. Instead, the two men exchanged greetings and necklaces. Cortés gave Montezuma a string of pearls. Montezuma presented Cortés with two necklaces made from red snail shells and gold.

It seemed to be a good beginning, but the meeting would lead to tragedy. Within two years, Montezuma would be dead, his magnificent capital destroyed, and millions of Native Americans would be conquered by the Spanish.

*Hernán Cortés (1485–1547) was a Spanish soldier and adventurer who conquered the mighty Aztec empire. His **expedition** paved the way for Spanish rule of Mexico.*

Conqueror of Mexico

Hernán Cortés was a soldier, an explorer, a commander, and an adventurer. In his lifetime he inspired not only great devotion but also great hatred. He came to power at a time when Spain was extending its empire around the world. Christopher Columbus's discovery of the New World had opened up vast new areas for European empires to **exploit.** Cortés's expedition to Mexico greatly expanded Spain's lands and influence there. When he entered Tenochtitlán, becoming the first European to do so, it marked the beginning of the end for the once-powerful Aztec empire.

Montezuma II (1466–1520) was emperor of the Aztecs when Cortés arrived in Mexico in 1519. During his rule, the empire reached its greatest extent. His death caused a massive uprising against the Spanish.

THE GREATEST CONQUISTADOR?

Cortés was a **conquistador**—one of the brave, tough, and ruthless Spanish soldiers who conquered vast areas of North and South America in the 1500s. (*Conquistador* is a Spanish word meaning "conqueror.") The conquistadors wanted to gain gold for their country and glory for themselves, and also to **convert** people to Christianity. Many conquistadors were the first Europeans to enter the regions they explored. Besides Cortés, some other famous conquistadors were Francisco Pizarro, who conquered the Incas of Peru; Hernando de Soto, who explored much of what is now the southeastern United States; and Juan Ponce de León, who explored present-day Florida in his search for the Fountain of Youth.

Childhood in Spain

Hernán Cortés was born in 1485, at a time when the Spanish didn't even know that North and South America existed. His parents, Martín Cortés de Monroy and **Doña** Catalina Pizarro Altamarino, both came from old, respected Spanish families. However, they were no longer rich. Years later, Cortés's secretary would write: "They had little wealth, but much honor." Young Hernán grew up in a town called Medellín, in central Spain. Like most upper-class Spanish boys at that time, Cortés was taught to fight with a sword and ride a horse. He did both expertly.

> **In the words of a biographer:**
>
> *"As an infant, Hernán Cortés was so frail that many times he was on the point of dying."*
>
> Francisco López de Gómara wrote a biography of Cortés.

Cortés grew up at a time when Spain was a growing power. In 1492, when Cortés was eight, Spanish soldiers captured Granada, the last Moorish stronghold in Spain. The **Moors,** who had ruled much of Spain for centuries, were forced to leave. The whole country celebrated the great victory. Then came news of Columbus's voyage. It seemed that another world lay open to Spanish conquest.

The town of Medellín lies in a region called Extremadura, which was the home of many of the most famous conquistadors. The castle overlooking the town was there in Cortés's time, and now there is also a statue of the town's most famous resident.

A change in plans

At first, however, Cortés didn't plan to become a soldier. His father encouraged him to study law, and Cortés attended the university at Salamanca. But after two years Cortés either found his studies too hard or too boring, and he left. He was tired of small-town life, and the stories of riches and adventure in the New World fascinated him. Cortés became determined to make his own fortune. After spending some time in Spain's southern port cities, meeting and talking to travelers returning from the New World, he left Spain in 1504 and sailed to the island of Hispaniola. He was nineteen years old.

THE "NEW WORLD"

In 1492, an Italian named Christopher Columbus led three ships into the Atlantic Ocean. Columbus hoped to find a short, direct route to the **Indies.** These lands were home to valuable spices that were in great demand in Europe. Whoever discovered an easy sea route to the Indies would become rich. In October, a lookout spotted land. Columbus thought he had landed in the Indies, so he called the people he saw "Indians." But he was wrong. He had run into a land mass unknown to the Europeans—North and South America. Over the next decades, many Spanish followed Columbus's route to what they called the "New World."

To the New World

Cortés's first years in North America were unremarkable. When he arrived on the island of Hispaniola in the Caribbean Sea, he settled in a town called Azúa. For the next several years, he tried his hand at farming, trading, and mining. Illness kept him from joining an **expedition** to South America in 1509.

For the most part, Cortés lived quietly. He became friends with **Don** Diego Velázquez de Cuéllar, the local Spanish ruler. Cortés joined Velázquez's expedition to conquer nearby Cuba. After this successful campaign, Velázquez became governor of Cuba and gave Cortés a large farm, mines, and Indian slaves. For the next thirteen years, Cortés spent most of his time developing his land.

Then, in 1518, Cortés received the opportunity of a lifetime. A Spanish expedition reported that a large land existed west of Cuba. Even more important, the Spanish ships returned with pieces of gold. When Velázquez heard the news, he threw a party that lasted eight days.

Dreaming of wealth and power, Velázquez quickly organized another expedition. He named Cortés as commander and ordered him to travel to these lands, spread Christianity among the Indians, and find gold.

*Don Diego Velázquez de Cuéllar (1465–1524) sailed to the New World in 1493 on Christopher Columbus's second voyage. He later became an important **mentor** for Hernán Cortés.*

In the sixteenth century, when Cortés traveled, ships were not built for comfort. Long ocean voyages could be cramped and uncomfortable.

Captain Cortés

Being named captain of an expedition seemed to change Cortés. He began to dress more carefully, and he carried himself with more pride. He recruited men, bought supplies, and found ships. Velázquez noticed the change nervously. He had hoped to be able to control Cortés easily, especially if Cortés discovered riches. Now, Cortés appeared to be quite willing to take charge on his own.

After several months, Velázquez decided to replace Cortés with another commander. But by then it was too late. Cortés had assembled 6 ships, more than 500 men, and enough supplies for a long voyage. By November the men were loaded onto the ships, and smoked meat, wine, water, and bread were stowed belowdecks. Velázquez rushed down to the harbor, arriving just in time to see Cortés and his ships leave.

To Mexico

You can follow Cortés's expedition on the map on pages 42–43.

Cortés and his **expedition** sailed along the coast of Cuba, taking on more supplies and convincing men to join his adventure. By the time he left Cuba in February 1519, Cortés led 11 ships with about 530 men, 8 women, and 17 horses.

Cortés commanded an impressive army, including 30 men armed with **crossbows.** Another twelve had **harquebuses,** an early type of gun that looked like a musket. Many of the rest had steel swords or spears. Cortés also had several cannons and a weapon few Native Americans had ever seen—horses. He also brought along metal bells, glass beads, mirrors, clothing, scissors, knives, and axes. He would give these as gifts to the people he met.

Battle at Potonchan

At first, Cortés had little opportunity to exchange gifts. The expedition reached the Mexican coast and stopped at Potonchan, where the Tabascans lived. There, Tabascans in canoes paddled around the ships and made threatening gestures. Cortés said he only wanted to draw fresh water and trade for food. But the Tabascans didn't trust him and told him to stay away.

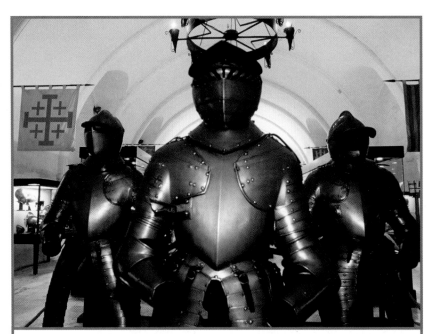

*The metal armor worn by many **conquistadors** was heavy and clumsy, but it provided good protection against swords and arrows.*

After defeating a group of Tabascan warriors, Cortés and his soldiers drove the Tabascans out of Potonchan. The next day, Cortés divided his force. While the Spanish **infantry** and gunmen fought the Tabascan warriors on foot, Cortés led fifteen horsemen in a surprise assault from the rear.

Victory

The Tabascans were brave warriors, but they were no match for the **cavalry.** The horsemen whirled and slashed at them while volleys of Spanish gunfire crashed into them. By the end of the day, the Tabascan army was crushed. Their chiefs arrived the next day to make peace.

The height and speed of their horses gave the Spanish a great advantage over the Native Americans.

The battle showed that Cortés and his troops could fight well. But Cortés was also generous in victory and quick to forget grudges. He rarely fought unless it was completely necessary, preferring to use his **cunning** and speaking ability to get what he wanted.

Important messengers

After the victory, Cortés led his ships north to a spot called San Juan de Ulúa. Members of the Totonac tribe appeared in canoes to greet them. The next day, Cortés and a party rowed ashore. The Totonacs welcomed them, giving them food, including a dish not known in Spain: turkey.

On Easter Sunday, 1519, Cortés met with messengers from a different tribe. They tried to speak, but Cortés and his **interpreter** could not understand them. Frustrated, Cortés noticed that a young Tabascan woman was chatting with the messengers. The woman, Malinche, spoke both Náhuatl (the Aztec language) and Mayan, the language of the peoples who lived along the coast.

Cortés ordered her to begin **translating** for him. With the help of Malinche and another Spaniard who spoke Mayan, he learned that the strangers were messengers from the Aztec **empire.** Their leader, they said, was called Montezuma.

The Aztec Empire

Although Cortés had never heard of him, Montezuma ruled the greatest and richest **empire** in the Americas. Home to four million people, it stretched from the Pacific Ocean to the Gulf of Mexico, across the lands that now make up the country of Mexico.

At its heart was Tenochtitlán, the magnificent Aztec capital city. The Aztecs built the first structures of Tenochtitlán on a tiny island in the middle of Lake Texcoco. The lake was in a valley surrounded by snowcapped mountains. The Aztecs marked off giant squares by driving wooden stakes into the shallow lake waters. They then filled in the squares with dirt and rocks, creating new land. As the city grew to 200,000 inhabitants, its size and strength terrified the surrounding peoples.

The Aztecs built houses out of stone and **adobe** bricks made from dried mud. When a house was finished, it was then painted white, and the entire city seemed to gleam in the sun.

Diego Rivera, a famous Mexican artist, painted many murals that showed the glory of Tenochtitlán at the height of the Aztec empire.

Causeways of earth and stone, about 20 feet (6 meters) wide, connected the city to the shore. The causeways were connected by several bridges. In times of war, the bridges could be raised.

One of the most important Aztec gods was the sun god. Here, a sacrifice is being offered on a calendar stone.

The Aztecs used canoes to carry food, crafts, and other items into the city, where they traveled on a network of canals. Because the lake water was not fit for drinking, the Aztecs built an **aqueduct** of clay pipes that carried fresh water from a spring into Tenochtitlán.

War and religion

The Aztecs raised their sons to be warriors. From an early age, Aztec boys learned to use bows and arrows, spears, and oak swords rimmed with razor-sharp volcanic stone. After the age of ten, Aztec boys wore a single lock of hair. They could only cut their hair after capturing a prisoner.

Taking a prisoner was the greatest feat for an Aztec warrior. The prisoners were then killed, or **sacrificed,** in religious ceremonies. The sacrifices were performed on pyramids that rose high above the city. The Aztecs believed that if they did not offer sacrifices of human flesh and blood to the gods, their society would be destroyed.

MONTEZUMA'S ZOO

Montezuma had a large zoo in Tenochtitlán. Its wooden cages held lions, jaguars, tigers, and wolves. Snakes were kept in large clay pots. Montezuma also kept two large aviaries for birds and more than 300 servants to care for them. The most colorful feathers were reserved for the emperor himself.

Montezuma's Fear

You can follow Cortés's expedition on the map on pages 42–43.

While Cortés and his men listened to the Aztec messengers, Montezuma was trying to learn about Cortés. He had heard reports that white, bearded strangers had been spotted on the coast. Curious and anxious, he sent messengers to find out who the strangers were and why they had come to his land.

Disturbing signs

Montezuma was a priest as well as **emperor**. He was troubled by some disturbing signs that had been seen before the strangers' arrival. In 1502, the Aztecs had observed

> **In the words of an Aztec:**
>
> *"The animals they rode—they looked like deer—were as high as roof tops."*
>
> One Aztec report had this to say about the Spaniards' horses.

what they called a "tongue of fire" in the night sky—a brilliant comet that blazed for more than a year. An **astrologer** warned Montezuma that it meant disaster.

In spring of 1519, a man from the coast told Montezuma that he had recently seen strange things: "a range of mountains, or some big hills, floating in the sea." A close adviser hurried to the coast and soon returned with bad news. It was true—a mysterious group of men was floating on two towers on the water.

This Aztec painting shows Montezuma's spies watching Cortés's ships about to land.

"The skins of these people are white, much more so than our own skins are," said the adviser. "All of them have long beards and hair down to their ears."

Meeting the strangers

Montezuma sent his most trusted adviser, Teudile, with gifts for the strangers. He hoped they would take the gifts, leave, and never return. Teudile greeted Cortés and presented him with gold jewelry, large quantities of food, and thousands of servants. Cortés liked the gifts, but he was most pleased by the sight of the gold. Relying on Malinche to **translate,** Cortés offered Teudile gifts of his own: beads, a silk coat, a chair, and a red hat with a golden medal.

The Aztec god Quetzalcoatl was often shown as a feathered snake. According to legend, he sailed east on a raft made of snakes.

Teudile was fascinated by the Spaniards' iron helmets, which he thought resembled the headdress worn by an Aztec god. Cortés let him send a helmet to Montezuma, but only if Montezuma returned it filled with grains of gold. The Aztecs drew pictures of the Spanish soldiers, their cannons, and their horses. Teudile sent these reports on to Montezuma. "If the cannon is aimed against a mountain, the mountain splits and cracks open," read one report.

Men or gods?

Montezuma wondered if the strangers were gods. According to Aztec legend, the god Quetzalcoatl had sailed east into the Sun, promising that he would return to rule Tenochtitlán. Worse, 1519 was the Aztec year One Reed, the year Quetzalcoatl was supposed to return. Some legends described the god as a bearded man.

Montezuma considered the problem for a while before deciding, with his advisers, that the Spanish should not come to Tenochtitlán.

Don't Come to Tenochtitlán

YOU CAN FOLLOW CORTÉS'S EXPEDITION ON THE MAP ON PAGES 42–43.

Montezuma sent a message to Cortés through Teudile. Unfortunately, the two could not meet, said Teudile. Montezuma could not travel to Cortés, and Cortés should not attempt to come to Tenochtitlán. The way was long, difficult, and dangerous, he said.

Hoping to convince the Spanish to leave, Montezuma included several more gifts with his message. The most spectacular of them were two disks, each 6 feet (2 meters) in diameter. One was made of silver, the other of gold. Cortés and his men were thrilled by these signs of Aztec wealth.

Cortés insisted that he had to see Montezuma. If he did not, he explained, his king would be angry at him. Teudile delivered Cortés's reply to Montezuma, who ordered Teudile to return to Cortés. Teudile did, bringing more gifts. This time, more firmly, Teudile told Cortés that he could not see Montezuma. Cortés should leave immediately.

MALINCHE

Cortés was a good speaker, but he needed someone to **translate.** His translator, Malinche, would stay at Cortés's side throughout his travels. She was his voice. After becoming a Christian, she changed her name to Doña Marina. Later, she and Cortés had a son. Marina's reputation has suffered over time. Today, she is largely considered a traitor. Because she was loyal to Cortés, she is blamed for helping destroy the Indians of North and South America.

After finishing, Teudile left, taking with him the thousands of Indians that had acted as servants to the Spanish. No more food was delivered.

The site of Villa Rica de la Vera Cruz is now home to a small fishing village. The modern city of Veracruz, Mexico, is a short distance away from Cortés's original town. It was moved to its present location in 1599.

Several members of Cortés's group argued that they should return to Cuba. Supplies were low, food was scarce, and some of the Spanish were worried about the obvious wealth and power of the Aztecs.

Villa Rica de la Vera Cruz

Cortés faced a difficult decision, but he did not consider returning to Cuba. Instead, on June 28, he founded a town called Villa Rica de la Vera Cruz on the Mexican coast. He instructed his men to lay out streets and build a strong wall for defense. Not surprisingly, Cortés was elected mayor of the new town, and his **allies** were named to the highest positions.

Cortés also reached out to local tribes. As the Spanish marched to the site of Villa Rica de la Cruz, they met Totonacs from the town of Cempoallan. The chief, reportedly a man so fat he could hardly move, welcomed Cortés and his men with a banquet and gifts. Later, Cortés and the chief, named Tlacochcalcatl, discussed the Aztecs. Tlacochcalcatl complained that the Aztecs took his food as **tribute** and seized many of his people as slaves.

Cortés listened closely and realized that the Aztecs had many enemies. He quickly made Tlacochcalcatl an ally.

Conquer or Die

You can follow Cortés's expedition on the map on pages 42–43.

After a comfortable two-week stay, Cortés and his men left Cempoallan. Tlacochcalcatl gave the Spanish more than 400 men to carry their supplies and equipment. At the next city, Quiahuiztlan, the Spanish were again welcomed. The chief of Quiahuiztlan also complained about Aztec rule.

Almost at the same time as the Spanish arrived, Aztec **nobles** arrived at Quiahuiztlan to take **tribute.** They entered the city dressed in magnificent clothing and sniffing flowers that only the upper classes were allowed to smell. Servants surrounded the officials and shooed away flies.

Cortés's plan

Cortés told the chief of Quiahuiztlan to put the Aztec nobles in prison, a suggestion that terrified the chief. But he finally agreed, and the officials were tied to poles and placed under Spanish guard.

That night, Cortés showed his **cunning.** He ordered two of the Aztec officials be brought to him. In the darkness, Cortés told the officials that he wanted to be friends with Montezuma and that they should meet. Cortés then ordered the two officials to be released. They hurried back to Tenochtitlán.

The Aztecs were famous for their beautiful featherwork. This fan probably belonged to Montezuma.

Many of Cortés's men were frightened by his order to destroy the ships. They now had no way of returning to Cuba.

More messengers soon arrived from Montezuma. They said he was pleased that Cortés had released two of his officials. A meeting was possible.

No way out

Cortés was determined to travel to Tenochtitlán. But some of his officers still hoped to avoid making such a dangerous journey. They plotted to steal a ship and return to Cuba. When Cortés discovered the plan, he ordered harsh punishment. Two men were hanged, and another had his foot cut off. Several were whipped.

To crush any more plots, Cortés ordered nine of his twelve ships to be stripped of their sails and **beached** on a sandbar. As his men looked on in shock, the ships broke apart and sank. Only one option remained: Tenochtitlán. We must "conquer or die," Cortés told them.

The Tlaxcalans

YOU CAN FOLLOW CORTÉS'S EXPEDITION ON THE MAP ON PAGES 42–43.

In August 1519, Cortés led his army of soldiers and Native American **porters** into the dense forests and cornfields that lay along Mexico's coast. The region was hot and humid, and the **expedition** was frequently soaked by summer rains.

The army stopped briefly about 50 miles (80 kilometers) from the coast, at a town called Jalapa. Here the forests thinned as the land rose to 6,000 feet (1,830 meters) above sea level. The muggy summer air turned cool and clear. The expedition stopped at a city called Zautla. As ordered by Montezuma, the Zautla chief gave the Spanish food, water, and shelter.

Tlaxcala

After resting for several days, Cortés led his men into Tlaxcala, a remote area not ruled by Montezuma. The Tlaxcalans were fierce warriors who fought regularly with the Aztecs. Remarkably, they had not been conquered. Cortés hoped to make them **allies,** but the first meeting did not go well. After following some Tlaxcalan scouts, the Spanish ran into a giant army. A battle followed, and the Spanish used their **cavalry** to scatter the Tlaxcalan warriors. Still, two horses were killed, and Cortés's plan to win new allies appeared to be ruined.

Cortés's army was not large enough to intimidate the Native Americans by size alone, but their horses, armor, and weapons had never been seen before.

Cortés sent messengers to Tlaxcala, again stating that he came in peace. The Tlaxcalans considered this but decided to attack the Spanish anyway. They tied up Cortés's messengers and prepared them for **sacrifice.**

Cortés and his men continued their march toward the Tlaxcalan capital city. The Tlaxcalans assembled their entire army before the Spanish camp and attacked. The Tlaxcalan warriors' razor-edged swords shattered against the Spanish steel. On Cortés's orders, the horsemen aimed their lances at the Indians' eyes. The Spanish gun and cannon fire was too much for the Tlaxcalans. At the end of the day, they retreated.

The Tlaxcalans were some of the toughest fighters that Cortés and his men faced.

A costly victory

Even though Cortés's men had won, the battles had drained them of their energy and their confidence. More than 50 men had died so far from wounds or disease. Cortés himself was weak with a fever. Far from home and exhausted, some of the Spaniards asked Cortés to order a retreat to the coast. Cortés refused.

The Tlaxcalans were also discouraged by their defeats. The Spanish, despite their small numbers, had beaten them easily. The Tlaxcalan leaders decided that being friendly with the Spanish was better than fighting them. They sent messengers to Cortés, asking forgiveness and permission to join him. The messengers arrived with gifts of food and slaves. Cortés, with some relief, immediately accepted. Several days later, the Spanish entered the city of Tlaxcala and were greeted as friends.

Cholula

You can follow Cortés's expedition on the map on pages 42–43.

Cortés and his men rested in Tlaxcala for twenty days. Speaking through Marina, Cortés told the Tlaxcalan chiefs that he wished to help them. The Tlaxcalans, who had fought the Aztecs for decades, respected the Spaniards for their bravery and skill at warfare. Thousands of Tlaxcalan warriors eagerly joined the war against the hated Aztecs.

In Tenochtitlán, Montezuma was amazed to hear that the Spanish kept approaching. He ordered his guides to return to Tenochtitlán. His mood changed frequently. Sometimes, he appeared to be on the verge of panic. "What can we do? We are finished." Other times, he planned to do battle. "We must not hide nor flee nor show cowardice," he said. He ordered his **sorcerers** to put spells on Cortés and the Spanish, to stop them.

A bad beginning

The spells didn't work. Cortés soon marched to Cholula, a city that was a close Aztec **ally.** Cholula was one of the largest cities in North America, with the largest pyramid on the continent. The Tlaxcalans warned Cortés that Cholula was a trap.

The Cholulans did not come out to meet Cortés. Instead of supplies and shelter, the Spanish army received only a small amount of food and water. Cortés waited angrily as the city rulers said they were too ill to meet him.

In the modern town of Cholula, a Spanish church stands atop the ruins of an ancient pyramid.

Cortés also noticed that the Cholulans were piling stones on the roofs of their homes. Cortés, now suspecting an **ambush,** ordered the city's leader to appear. The chief told Cortés that Montezuma had ordered him not to give any food to the Spanish. He said that 20,000 Aztec warriors were waiting on the road to Tenochtitlán to slaughter the Spanish when they left Cholula.

When he took Cholula, Cortés conquered a city that had been an important cultural center for more than 1,000 years. The Cholulans were famous for their cloth and pottery.

Massacre at Cholula

Cortés called the leaders of Cholula together in a temple in the center of the city. When the doors were locked, Cortés accused them of **treason.** They protested, saying they were following the orders of Montezuma. When a signal gun was fired, the Spanish fell on the leaders, stabbing and killing them. The Tlaxcalans then **sacked** the city. The rows of homes and temples were burned.

> **In the words of an Aztec:**
>
> *"Clearly their thirst for gold was* **insatiable;** *they starved for it; they lusted for it; they wanted to stuff themselves with it as if they were pigs."*

Cortés then sent a message to Montezuma. Cortés said he would not enter Tenochtitlán in peace, but as an enemy at war. Montezuma's messengers protested and returned to Tenochtitlán. Montezuma sent Cortés ten plates of gold, cotton cloaks, and food. Through his messenger, Montezuma said he had known nothing about the ambush. He again begged Cortés and his men not to come to Tenochtitlán. But Cortés was too close to stop now.

Montezuma Meets Cortés

You can follow Cortés's expedition on the map on pages 42–43.

One last barrier remained until Tenochtitlán—a range of high mountains. As the Spanish reached the top of the mountain range, they saw a sight of breathtaking beauty. The Valley of Mexico spread out before them. A patchwork of cornfields surrounded a deep blue lake at the valley's center. In the lake was a giant city—Tenochtitlán.

Cortés and his army paused for a night at Iztapalapa, a town that was just a few miles from Tenochtitlán. On November 8, Cortés ordered his men to organize into a column and begin walking down the main **causeway** into Tenochtitlán. Thousands of Aztecs crowded the causeway and filled canoes on the lakes to watch.

Cortés and his men were impressed by the way the Aztecs used canals to transport people and goods.

First came the dogs, barking and scampering around the column. Then came four horsemen, their armor and swords flashing in the sunlight. A single man followed, carrying Cortés's banner. Spanish **infantry** and more horsemen came next. Then came the **crossbowmen** and gunmen. Cortés, surrounded by banners and **cavalry,** was in the rear. Thousands of Tlaxcalan warriors followed Cortés. They were painted for war and made shrieking and whistling sounds.

The Spanish were impressed by the size and beauty of Tenochtitlán. Most of them had never seen such a large city. At the spot where the causeway entered the city, the Spanish were greeted by a thousand Aztec **nobles.**

While Cortés waited, each Aztec noble kissed his hand and touched the ground as a sign of welcome. After an hour, the Spanish saw Aztec men sweeping the street with brooms. Next came two lines of colorfully dressed nobles and warriors, some of them wearing the skins of jaguars. Then, a man carried in a gold and silver chair and covered in green feathers and flowers appeared. It was Montezuma. Cortés dismounted from his horse. Montezuma descended from his chair.

Montezuma and Cortés greeted each other politely enough when they first met, but their relationship would soon turn sour.

After greeting Montezuma, Cortés and his men followed him to his palace. The streets and homes were crowded with curious Aztecs, eager for a glimpse of the strangers. Montezuma left Cortés and his men in comfortable rooms. "You are in your own house," Montezuma told Cortés. "So are your brothers. Rest."

Prisoner of the Spanish

You can follow Cortés's expedition on the map on pages 42–43.

As the Spanish explored Tenochtitlán, they were astonished by the maze of canals and narrow streets that suddenly opened into wide avenues. They were amazed by the vast marketplace, where thousands of Aztecs exchanged all kinds of goods—fruits, jewels, vegetables, slaves, chocolate, turkeys, and colorful cloths.

"With such wonderful sights to gaze on, we did not know what to say, or if this was real that we saw before our eyes," wrote one of the Spaniards, Bernal Díaz del Castillo.

Montezuma, Cortés, and several of his officers climbed the steep stairs of the tallest pyramid in Tenochtitlán. At the top, Montezuma asked Cortés if the climb had tired his companions. "Spaniards never tire," Cortés replied.

Despite the joking, Cortés was uncomfortable that his life and his men were in Montezuma's hands. The **emperor** was a good host for now. But with one word, Montezuma could order his warriors to have them killed.

Cortés demanded that Montezuma swear loyalty to his king, Charles V. When he did, Cortés was pleased. Cortés dreamed that Tenochtitlán would become an important part of the Spanish **empire**— a source of gold, jewels, and silver.

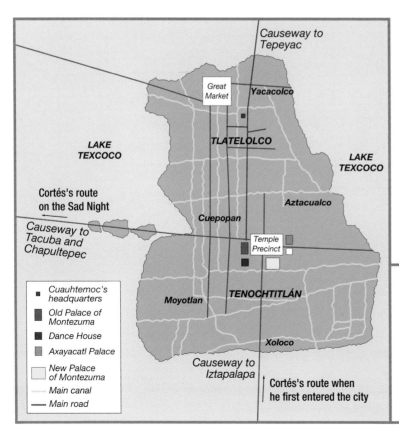

Cuauhtemoc's headquarters
Old Palace of Montezuma
Dance House
Axayacatl Palace
New Palace of Montezuma
Main canal
Main road

Causeway to Tepeyac
Great Market
Yacacolco
LAKE TEXCOCO
TLATELOLCO
LAKE TEXCOCO
Cortés's route on the Sad Night
Causeway to Tacuba and Chapultepec
Aztacualco
Cuepopan
Temple Precinct
Moyotlan
TENOCHTITLÁN
Xoloco
Causeway to Iztapalapa
Cortés's route when he first entered the city

The city of Tenochtitlán lay completely within the waters of Lake Texcoco. This map shows how the city was crisscrossed by roads and canals, and how it was connected to the mainland by causeways.

Taking Montezuma prisoner

Just five days after arriving in Tenochtitlán, Cortés received reports that the men he had left behind at Villa Rica de la Vera Cruz had been attacked by a local tribe. At least seven Spaniards had been killed. The next day, Cortés and 30 heavily armed men met with Montezuma at his palace. Cortés angrily showed the letter to Montezuma and accused him of **treachery.** Montezuma denied giving the orders.

Cortés demanded that Montezuma return with him to his palace and become his prisoner. Montezuma could still rule as before, but he could not leave without permission. If Montezuma refused, said Cortés, he would be killed immediately.

*The Aztecs received **tribute** from many tribes in the region. The Mixtecs, who provided this pendant, were well-known for their skill in working with gold.*

Montezuma must have been shocked by this proposal. For his entire life, the emperor had been waited on and his every word obeyed. Out of respect, his servants dared not even look him in the eye. But something about Cortés must have made a great impression on Montezuma, making him agree to Cortés's demand.

Montezuma's subjects, especially his warriors and **nobles,** were worried and angered. Worse, Cortés kept pressing Montezuma to become a Christian and stop **sacrificing** humans. He climbed the steps to the city's most important temple. Cortés walked before several small statues worshiped by the Aztecs. He ordered his men to remove the **idols** and clean the temple. The Spanish knocked down several walls and made the structure into a church. These actions angered the Aztec nobles, who began to grumble among themselves about the Spanish.

You can follow Cortés's expedition on the map on pages 42–43.

As tension grew in Tenochtitlán, Cortés learned that a Spanish **expedition** from Cuba had arrived off the coast of Mexico. Commanded by Pánfilo de Narváez, a force of 1,400 men had been sent by **Don** Diego Velázquez de Cuéllar to kill or capture Cortés. Narváez called Cortés an outlaw.

Montezuma heard of the landings, including the news that Cortés was a criminal. He was delighted, believing that Cortés would have to leave at last. But Cortés did not panic. He took about 150 men and marched to the coast. He left another 80 men in Tenochtitlán under the command of Pedro de Alvarado.

The Aztecs were fierce warriors, but they were unable to defend their city against Cortés and his army.

Cortés and his men advanced at night under the cover of a heavy storm. When the order came to attack, they swarmed out of the darkness, surprising Narváez and his men. After a fierce battle, Narváez was stabbed in the eye and captured. The rest of his men quickly surrendered. Cortés told Narváez's men about the wonders of Tenochtitlán and recruited them to his cause.

Massacre in Tenochtitlán

Cortés had won, but then came terrible news. In the days after Cortés left Tenochtitlán, Pedro de Alvarado had grown very nervous. His Native American **allies** told him that the Aztecs were planning to slaughter the Spanish and eat them. Alvarado watched fearfully as the Aztecs prepared for a great **sacrifice.**

Convinced that they would soon be killed, Alavarado plotted to strike first.

During the sacrifice ceremony, thousands of Aztec **nobles** gathered in the city square before the great pyramid. To the beating of giant drums, they danced and celebrated. After the ceremony had begun, Alvarado blocked the entrances to the square. Then the Spanish attacked the Aztec dancers and musicians. News of the **massacre** spread through the city, and Aztec warriors angrily demanded revenge. They surrounded the Spanish, who had taken shelter in a palace with Montezuma.

*The stone that killed Montezuma was probably thrown by one of his own people, but many Aztecs claimed that Cortés had murdered their **emperor.***

Cortés, in the meantime, returned to Tenochtitlán with 1,300 soldiers. He was shocked when he entered the city to find Alvarado and his men exhausted and almost starving. Cortés angrily demanded to know what had happened, but he knew that little could be done. The Aztecs were raising bridges from the **causeways.** The Spanish were trapped in the city.

Montezuma's death

Aztec warriors surrounded the Spanish in their palace. Whenever the Spanish tried to leave, Aztecs on nearby roofs threw stones at them. Desperate, the Spanish convinced Montezuma to climb a wall to calm his people. For a few moments, the city became silent as Montezuma spoke. But then he was showered with stones. In shock and bleeding from his wounds, he was carried back to his chamber. He refused to eat or drink and died within days.

The Sad Night

You can follow Cortés's expedition on the map on pages 42–43.

The Spanish and their **allies** fought on, but they were growing tired, hungry, and thirsty. As thousands of Aztec warriors filled the streets of Tenochtitlán, Cortés planned a desperate escape. Shortly after midnight on July 1, 1520, Cortés and his men put on their armor. Most of the massive gold treasure was loaded on horses. The rest of it was distributed among the men.

Under cover of darkness, the Spanish and about 100 Tlaxcalans tiptoed through the city streets and arrived at a **causeway.** There, an Aztec women spotted them and cried an alarm. The Aztecs soon surrounded the Spanish force, now strung out on the causeway, and showered them with stones and arrows.

The events of "La Noche Triste" were a bitter defeat for the Spaniards.

The bridges over the gaps in the causeways were torn up. The Spanish force became a disorganized mass. Some soldiers fell into the water, where they were weighed down by the gold in their pockets and drowned. Many Spanish soldiers were captured by the Aztecs, and more than 400 were killed. The Spanish called the disaster "La Noche Triste," meaning "sad night."

Retreat

Cortés's army, down to 400 men and 30 horses, retreated. Many of the men were wounded. All of them were hungry and exhausted. After ten days, the Spanish reached the friendly kingdom of Tlaxcala, where they rested for three weeks. Cortés, his skull fractured and two fingers **amputated,** would not accept defeat. Instead, he plotted to take Tenochtitlán once and for all.

Cortés surrounds Tenochtitlán

Over the next months, Cortés gathered reinforcements and supplies. Cortés knew that to conquer Tenochtitlán, he had to control the water around the city. He had to stop the Aztecs from carrying food and weapons in canoes. On April 28, 1521, he launched 12 ships that each carried about 25 soldiers. Carrying cannons and guns, the ships were powered by sails or oars and could move easily over the shallow waters of Lake Texcoco.

Return to the city

In May, Cortés ordered 86 **cavalry,** 118 **crossbowmen** and gunmen, 700 soldiers, and thousands of Tlaxcalans to split into 3 groups. One group went north to the city of Tacuba,

Gold from the New World flowed back to Spain to help finance wars and exploration. It was also used in buildings such as this cathedral in Tarragona.

where they broke the pipes that carried fresh water to Tenochtitlán. From then on, the Aztecs would have to rely on wells for water. Another force set out for the southern side of the lake and soon reached Iztapalapa, just across from the city.

On June 1, Cortés led his fleet of ships onto Lake Texcoco. Thousands of Aztecs came out in canoes to challenge him. The Spanish soldiers fired their cannons while the crossbowmen fired into the groups of canoes. The Aztecs were swept from the lake. Without control of the lake waters, Tenochtitlán was surrounded.

The Battle for Tenochtitlán

You can follow Cortés's expedition on the map on pages 42–43.

On three separate **causeways,** the Spanish and their Native American **allies** approached the city. The Aztec warriors resisted fiercely. The raised the bridges from the causeways, forcing the Spanish to cross the water-filled gaps. The Aztecs shot arrows, threw stones, and shouted insults. When the Spanish filled in a gap in the causeway, the Aztecs snuck out at night and dug it up. Aboard their ships, the Spanish charged into the city's canals and set fire to Aztec buildings.

Twice, the Spanish drove into the city's center but had to retreat. Aztec warriors used the houses as small fortresses and threw stones at the attackers from the roofs.

Cortés tried to negotiate for peace with the new **emperor,** Cuauhtemoc, but he scornfully refused. Stunned by the strong resistance, Cortés had to make a terrible decision. He did not want to destroy Tenochtitlán, a city he still regarded as the most beautiful in the world. It would do him no good as piles of rubble. But the Aztec warriors continued to fight. Reluctantly, Cortés ordered his men to burn the city as they advanced.

The Spanish and their **allies** fought their way through Tenochtitlán's streets. They burned buildings, filled in canals, and then left at night. The next day, they returned. The Aztec warriors resisted bitterly. When the

Cuauhtemoc was Montezuma's nephew as well as his son-in-law. His refusal to cooperate with the Spaniards made him a legend among the Aztecs.

Spanish retreated, the Aztecs dug up the causeways and canals once again. Despite having no food, little water, and no reinforcements, swarms of Aztec warriors awaited wherever the Spanish appeared.

A Spanish defeat

In July, the Aztecs dealt the Spanish a stinging setback. Three Spanish forces drove toward the center of the city. To cross a canal, the Spanish laid reeds on the water and walked across one at a time. On the other side, thousands of Aztecs **ambushed** them, and the Spanish fled. But when the soldiers tried to recross the reeds all at once, the plants sank under their weight. Panicked, the Spanish soldiers sank into the water as the Aztec warriors appeared on all sides.

One of the most important weapons for an Aztec warrior was the atlatl, or spear thrower. Both the atlatls shown here are covered in gold, and they are shown from the back so you can see the groove where the spear was placed.

Cortés, on the other side of the canal, tried to help. Spanish and Tlaxcalan soldiers soon jammed the muddy streets. Aztec warriors crossed the canal in canoes and joined the attack. Suddenly, Cortés found himself on foot and desperately fighting to escape. The Spanish, now little more than a mob, retreated to a causeway. At least 50 had been captured.

Later that evening, the Aztecs began pounding drums. As Cortés and his men watched in horror, the captured Spanish soldiers were paraded and made to dance atop the Aztec temple. Then their hearts were cut out by Aztec priests and their bodies thrown down the temple steps. Cortés and his commanders discussed furiously what had gone wrong. For the next four days, the Aztecs celebrated.

Resistance Crumbles

You can follow Cortés's expedition on the map on pages 42–43.

After the defeat, the Spanish stayed in the conquered parts of the city and rested for several weeks. Meanwhile, the Aztecs were growing weaker. The Spanish ships still kept food and reinforcements from reaching the city. The wells were running dry. The warriors were exhausted after months of battle. Some Aztecs began eating grass and straw to stay alive.

Again, Cortés appealed to Cuauhtemoc for peace. But the Aztec leader was determined to keep fighting. The Spanish and Tlaxcalans pushed the survivors into a tiny corner of the city.

On August 13, after 75 days of **siege,** the last Aztec resistance collapsed. Cuauhtemoc was captured as he fled the shattered city in a canoe. Cortés had Cuauhtemoc brought before him. When Cortés praised him for defending his city with such courage, Cuauhtemoc begged Cortés to kill him.

It was one of the most astonishing victories in history. A small band of Spanish soldiers and their Native American **allies** had conquered the Aztec **empire** and reduced its greatest city, Tenochtitlán, to ruins. At least 100,000 Aztecs had died in the battles with the Spanish.

This painting of the capture of Cuauhtemoc now hangs in the British Embassy in Mexico City.

Where is the gold?

For the next few days, the Spanish were not concerned with history. They wanted to find the gold that had been lost on the Sad Night. They searched for it frantically. Cuauhtemoc stayed mostly silent, even when the Spanish tortured him. When he finally said that the treasure had been thrown into a part of the lake, some Spanish soldiers quickly dove to the bottom but uncovered little.

The Spanish never found the vast treasure they had lost on the Sad Night. Cortés divided the remaining gold among himself, his captains, and set aside some for the king. So little was left for the common soldiers that they threatened to rebel. To calm them, Cortés offered them land and Native American slaves.

After taking down many of the Aztec idols, Cortés had his men replace them with Catholic images. This statue was replaced by one of the Virgin Mary.

The Spanish also took comfort by celebrating. Cortés heard that a ship full of pigs and wine had arrived in Villa Rica de la Vera Cruz. He ordered the cargo to be brought immediately to Tenochtitlán. After months of eating cornmeal tortillas and turkey, the Spanish gorged themselves on pork and wine.

Governor Cortés

After the Spanish had finished celebrating their victory, Cortés decided to build a new capital on the rubble of the beautiful city he had destroyed. Using the Aztecs as workers, he directed the construction of a giant cathedral near the site of Tenochtitlán's great pyramid.

Cortés hoped to impress the king of Spain with his feats. He packed three ships full of treasure, including jeweled masks, animal skin shields, and **idols** made of solid gold. He also sent a letter in which he described his adventures. The ships, however, were captured off the coast of North Africa and sent to the king of France.

More plans

In the meantime, Cortés continued to rule Mexico. He knew that the Pacific Ocean lay to the south and west. He planned to build shipyards and harbors in order to bring the riches of the **Indies** to Mexico and then to Spain.

But not everything was going well. Cortés's soldiers kept looking for gold. When they found little, they began to suspect that Cortés was keeping it for himself. Angry notes soon appeared

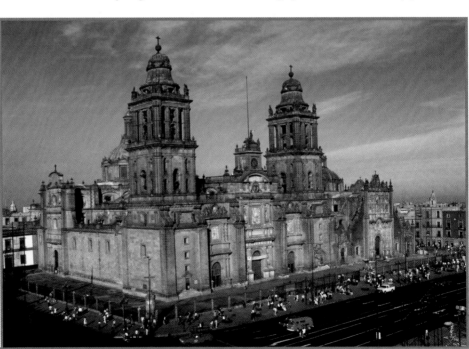

Cortés's men built a cathedral on the ruins of the Aztec temple. It was much smaller than the one that is there now, which was begun in 1572.

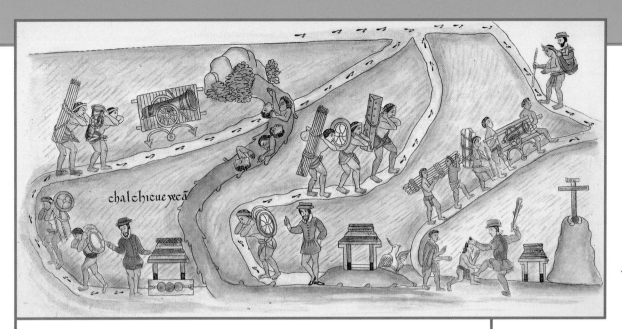

After the conquest of Mexico, many Native Americans were forced to work as slaves for the Spaniards. They were often used to carry heavy loads.

on Cortés's whitewashed palace walls. "How sad will my spirit be till Cortés has given back all the gold which he has taken," read one.

Cortés had other problems. He kept waiting for acknowledgment of his successes to come from Spain. Finally, in the summer of 1523, Cortés received letters from the king. He was appointed governor of Mexico. Cortés now concerned himself with dividing Mexico into estates, putting down **rebellions,** and building Mexico City.

Enemies of Cortés were worried that he might establish Mexico as an independent kingdom. Cortés was popular enough as a ruler that he might have been able to do it. But he had been brought up in a world that demanded absolute loyalty to the king, so he did not. He wrote five long letters to Charles V that explained his position in Mexico.

CATALINA

Cortés's first wife, Catalina, traveled from Spain to Mexico after her husband's victory. The visit was a surprise. Malinche was having Cortés's son at about the same time. Still, Cortés welcomed Catalina and she lived with him at his palace. Several months after her arrival, Catalina went to bed after a night of dancing and suddenly died. Some people suggested that Cortés had killed his wife in a fit of rage, but Cortés denied the rumors.

Later Years

YOU CAN FOLLOW CORTÉS'S LAST EXPEDITION ON THE MAP ON PAGE 43.

As ruler, Cortés faced more problems. Many Spanish settlers arrived in Mexico, seeking gold and land. Others tried to unseat Cortés as ruler. In the following years, Cortés became involved in several legal disputes.

Cortés also still worried about Native American **rebellions.** In 1525, he suspected that Cuauhtemoc was plotting to lead a revolt, and he ordered him to be hanged.

Even though he was the ruler of Mexico City, Cortés grew restless. He led an **expedition** of more than 1,000 men into Honduras. After two years of fighting starvation and disease, Cortés and the rest of his expedition emerged from the jungle with fewer than 100 survivors. Cortés was shocked to learn that Mexico City had been taken over by others. He also learned that his enemies in Spain were turning the king against him.

Finally, in 1528, Cortés decided to sail to Spain and speak to the king himself. When Cortés arrived, he was given parades and celebrations. King Charles awarded him honors and appointed him to the order of the knights of Saint James. Delighted with the attention and fortune, Cortés returned to Mexico in 1530 with a new wife—a duchess named **Doña** Juana de Zuñiga.

When Cortés returned to Spain, he was hailed as a hero. Here he is greeted by crowds on the streets of Toledo, Spain.

Cortés died here, at the Castle of Cuesta in Seville, in 1547. Years of fame and fortune had led to a later life full of disappointment.

Final years

Cortés continued exploring and paid for expeditions into the Pacific Ocean. Perhaps, he thought, he might find the route to China. None of these efforts were successful.

As the years passed, Cortés and Juana had a son and three daughters. Cortés continued to rule Mexico. However, he still had many enemies in Spain. Again, Cortés felt he had to travel there to defend himself.

But times had changed. Cortés's conquest didn't excite the Spanish as it used to. Some even criticized Cortés for his brutal treatment of the Native Americans. Even the king no longer seemed to want Cortés at his court.

In 1544, Cortés settled near Seville, Spain. Three years later, on December 2, 1547, at the age of 63, he died. After several decades, his body was brought to Mexico City and laid to rest at the Hospital de Jesús.

In the words of an Aztec:

"Is it not enough that we have already lost? That our way of living has been lost, has been annihilated?"

When Christian priests tried to convert the Aztecs, many Aztec priests protested.

Cortés's Legacy

Even after his death, Cortés would not rest in peace. In the early 1800s, Mexicans revolted against Spain. Because Cortés represented Spanish conquest, his bones were hidden out of fear that they would be destroyed. Cortés's remains were stashed away again in the early 1900s because another revolution threatened them. For many years, they appeared to be lost. Finally, in 1946, a student discovered Cortés's bones in a hospital wall.

A mixed legacy

Today, Cortés is remembered both as a great adventurer and a great villain. To many in modern Mexico, he was a brutal and ruthless conqueror. He destroyed a civilization and brought millions of Native Americans under Spanish rule.

But Cortés was also brave and brilliant. Despite his willingness to use the sword, he avoided fighting whenever he could, preferring instead to negotiate. He forged a relationship— possibly even a friendship—with Montezuma.

This bust of Hernán Cortés, from the Hospital de Jesús in Mexico City, is the only statue of him in that city. He is viewed by many Mexicans as the destroyer of Aztec culture.

He also regretted destroying Tenochtitlán, a city he regarded as the most beautiful in the world. Some historians say Cortés built Mexico City partly to restore the glory of Tenochtitlán.

Cortés has also been blamed for the decline of Native American populations after the conquest. This resulted less from Spanish weapons than from disease. Cortés was also blamed for the Spanish abuse of Native Americans. Much of that reputation was deserved. But after 1528, Cortés took much greater care in how he treated the people he ruled.

Today, the Aztec culture lives on in Mexico. The Mexican flag carries the image of an eagle sitting on a cactus, with a snake grasped in its beak. The image comes from an Aztec myth. More than one million Mexicans still speak the Aztec language, Náhuatl.

In Mexico City, workmen building a subway in 1978 discovered the ruins of Tenochtitlán's greatest pyramid. Today, it is being excavated and preserved—a living part of Mexico's history. The only statue of Cortés in Mexico City, however, is not displayed in a public square, but hidden away in the Hospital de Jesús.

One of Cortés's most lasting legacies can be found in the modern population of Mexico. After conquering the Aztecs, many Spanish soldiers married Mexican women, mixing the two cultures.

THE WORST ATTACK OF ALL

The Indians suffered from Spanish brutality and rule, but the worst effect was one the Spanish didn't even intend—disease. Unprotected from European diseases—smallpox, measles, whooping cough, mumps—Indian populations were almost wiped out. Some historians estimate that the population of Indians in Mexico declined from 8 million in 1520 to about 2.5 million in 1560.

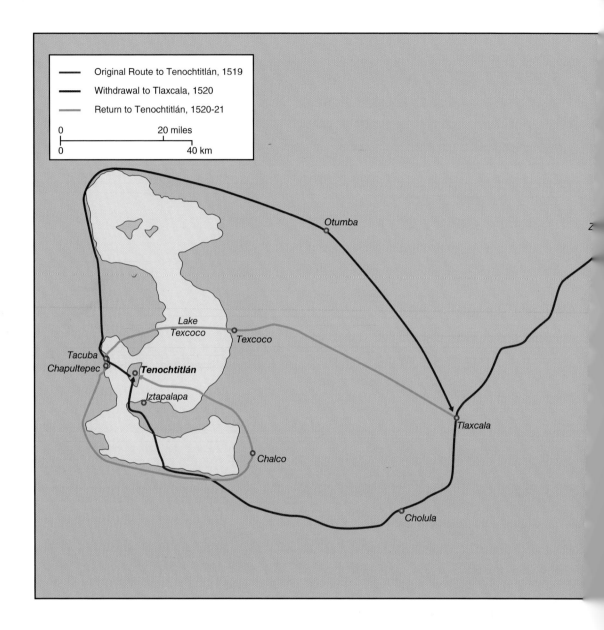

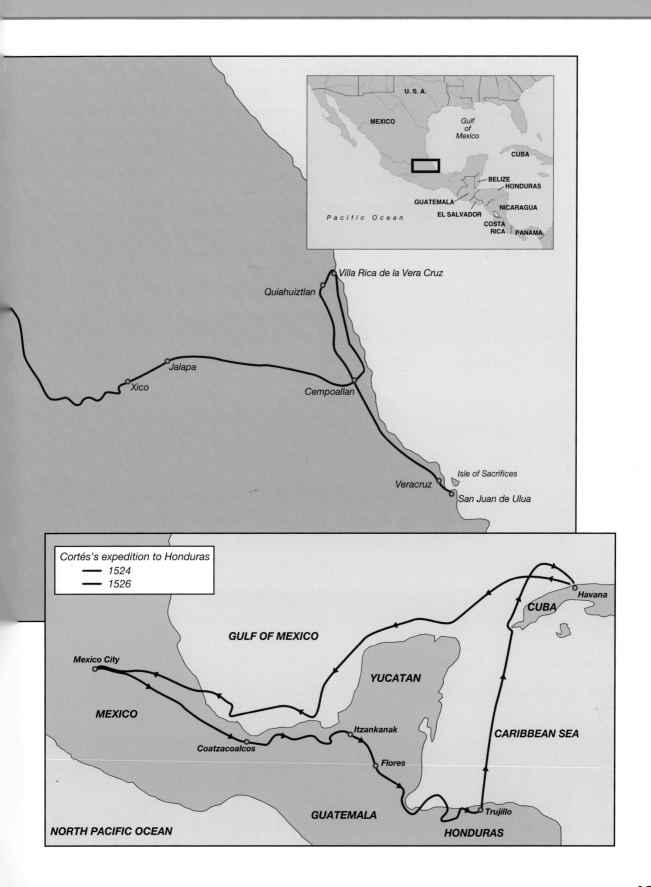

Villa Rica de la Vera Cruz

Quiahuiztlan

Jalapa

Xico

Cempoallan

Isle of Sacrifices

Veracruz

San Juan de Ulua

U. S. A.

MEXICO

Gulf of Mexico

CUBA

BELIZE

HONDURAS

GUATEMALA

NICARAGUA

EL SALVADOR

COSTA RICA

PANAMA

Pacific Ocean

Cortés's expedition to Honduras
1524
1526

GULF OF MEXICO

Mexico City

MEXICO

YUCATAN

Itzankanak

Coatzacoalcos

Flores

CARIBBEAN SEA

Havana

CUBA

GUATEMALA

HONDURAS

Trujillo

NORTH PACIFIC OCEAN

Timeline

1451 Christopher Columbus is born in Genoa, Italy.

1465 Diego Velázquez de Cuéllar is born.

1466 Montezuma is born.

1469 The marriage of Ferdinand and Isabella unites the Spanish kingdoms of Aragon and Castile, creating a stronger nation.

1485 Hernán Cortés is born in Medellín, Spain.

1492 Christopher Columbus, sailing for Spain, discovers the Americas while looking for a sea route to the **Indies.**

   The **Moors** are driven out of Spain.

1499 Cortés begins studying law at the University of Salamanca but leaves after two years.

1504 Cortés sails to the New World with Velázquez, landing in Hispaniola.

1509 Cortés is prevented by illness from going on an **expedition** to South America.

1511 Cortés joins an expedition to conquer Cuba.

1518 Cortés is appointed commander of an expedition to "New Spain."

1519 In February, Cortés leads a fleet to Mexico. He establishes contact with Montezuma, makes **allies** among the local tribes, and travels to Tenochtitlán. A group of soldiers, led by Pánfilo de Narváez, arrives from Cuba to arrest Cortés but is defeated in battle.

1520 Alvarado orders a **massacre** in Tenochtitlán. The Spanish are forced to retreat from the city, and Montezuma is killed. Cortés later returns to Tenochtitlán with an army.

1521 Tenochtitlán falls.

1524 Cortés leads an expedition to Honduras.

   Don Diego Velázquez de Cuéllar dies.

1528 Cortés returns to Spain to meet with the king.

1530   Cortés returns to New Spain. His first wife, Catalina, dies.

1532–5 Francisco Pizarro conquers the Incas in Peru.

1540   Cortés moves back to Spain.

Francisco Vásquez de Coronado leads an expedition to explore what is now the southwestern United States.

1542   Coronado's expedition returns to New Spain.

1547   Cortés dies on December 2, near Seville, Spain.

1823   After centuries of Spanish rule, a Mexican republic is declared.

1978   The ruins of an Aztec pyramid are discovered in Mexico City.

More Books to Read

Barghusen, Joan D. *The Aztecs: End of a Civilization.* Farmington Hills, Mich.: Gale Group, 2000.

Crisfield, Deborah. *Hernan Cortes.* Austin, Tex.: Raintree Steck-Vaughn Publishers, 2000.

Flowers, Charles. *Cortes and the Conquest of the Aztec Empire in World History.* Berkeley Heights, N.J.: Enslow Publishers, 2001.

Rees, Rosemary. *The Aztecs.* Chicago: Heinemann Library, 1999.

Wilson, Mike. *The Conquest of Mexico.* Broomall, Penn.: Mason Crest Publishers, 2002.

Glossary

adobe brick made of dried mud, used for building

ally someone united with another in a common purpose

ambush hidden place from which a surprise attack can be made

amputate to cut off, usually for medical reasons

annihilate to destroy completely

aqueduct structure that carries water from one place to another

astrologer person who tells fortunes based on the positions of the stars and planets

beach to run ashore

causeway raised road across water or wet ground

cavalry troops mounted on horseback

conquistador leader in the Spanish conquest of the Americas in the fifteenth and sixteenth centuries

crossbow weapon consisting of a bow mounted on a stock, which shoots short arrows

cunning cleverness in getting what one wants by using tricks or deception

Don Spanish title of respect, similar to "Sir." The female form is *Doña.*

emperor ruler of an empire

empire group of territories or peoples under one ruler

expedition trip taken to discover new places

exploit to make use of unfairly for one's own benefit

harquebus heavy, portable gun used by many soldiers in the fifteenth and sixteenth centuries

idol statue or image worshiped as a god

Indies old name for southeastern Asia, including India

infantry soldiers trained to fight on foot

insatiable unable to be satisfied

interpreter person who translates for someone else

massacre violent and cruel killing of a large number of people

mentor trusted person one can go to for advice, especially relating to one's career

Moor member of a Muslim people from North Africa who conquered Spain in the eighth century

noble person of high rank or birth

porter person who carries baggage for someone else

rebellion open fight by people against their government

sack to loot a city after capturing it

sacrifice act of making an offering to a god, sometimes by killing people or animals

siege act of surrounding a city or fort, often for a long time, in order to capture it

sorcerer person who practices magic or witchcraft

translate to change from one language to another

treachery betrayal of trust

treason crime of trying to overthrow a government or ruler

tribute payment by one ruler or nation to another, either given in return for protection or taken by force

Index